THE ABC's OF GOD

Written By
Peggy Wescott

Illustrated By
Mallory Root

AUTHOR'S DEDICATION

This book was written in
gratitude to my parents,
Margaret and Joseph Kolinski,
who, through their loving word
and example,
first introduced me to
the wonder and greatness of God.

ILLUSTRATOR'S DEDICATION

This book was designed for my parents,
who have always encouraged me to
achieve my dreams.
They have faithfully taught me
the word of God and helped me lay
a firm foundation on which to grow.
This work of art was a dream come true.
Thank you mom and dad.

Aa

Our God is
AWESOME; ALWAYS AFFIRMATIVE
and **AFFECTIONATE;**
ALL knowing and **ALL** loving.

Lord, our Lord,
how awesome is your name
through all the Earth!
-Ps 8:2

Bb

God is
BEYOND BELIEVABLE;
almost too good to be true,
but God is true.

Lord you have
probed my heart,
you know when
I sit and when I stand...

Such knowledge
is beyond me,
far too lofty
for me to
reach.
Ps 139:1,2,6

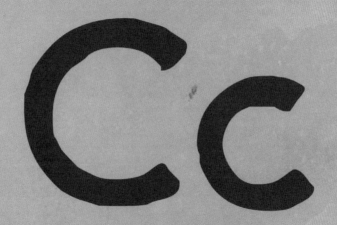

Cc

God is our CREATOR.
God made us
in his image; that means
we're very good, just like Him.

God created man
in his image;
in the divine image
he created him;
man and female
he created them.
Gn 1:27

Dd

God is
DEPENDABLE.
You can always count on God
to answer your prayers.

Ee

God is
EXCEPTIONAL,
EXCELLENT,
AND EMBRACEABLE;
EVERYTHING you hope a God could be.
God is there for
EVERYONE.

God is
EVERYWHERE.
God is ETERNAL.

Ff

God is FAITHFUL.
He's always there for us.
He's like a wonderful FATHER.
God is a FRIEND who will
help us make good choices.

Lord, your love
reaches to heaven;
your fidelity to the clouds.
- Ps 36:6

Gg

God is
GOOD and GENEROUS.
God is
GREAT!

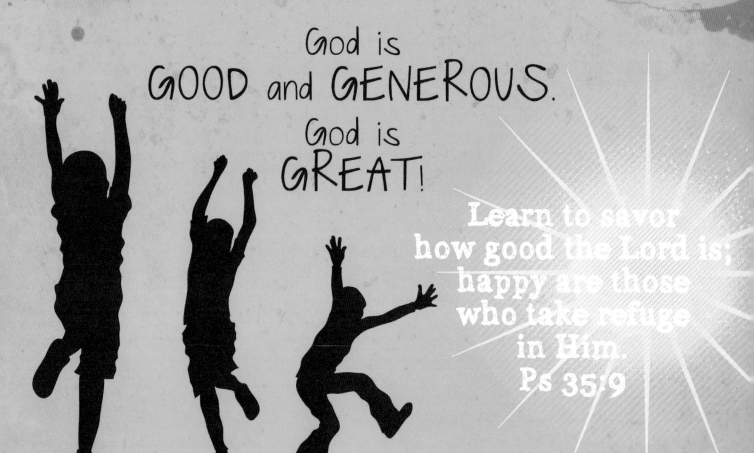

Learn to savor
how good the Lord is;
happy are those
who take refuge
in Him.
Ps 35:9

Hh

God is
HELPFUL.
God won't let any HARM
come to His Children.

You are my
help and my
deliverer;
my God,
do not delay!
- Ps 40:18

God is our
INSPIRATION.
God INSPIRES
us to be the best
we can be.

I can do
all things
through Christ
who strengthens me.
-Php 4:13

You shall love the Lord your God with all your heart, all your soul, all your strength, and all your mind. Also you must love your neighbor as yourself.
- Lk 10:27

God sent us
JESUS,
his Son.

JESUS

taught us to be
JOYFUL and JUST.

I made no secret
of Your enduring
kindness to a
great assembly.
Ps 40:11

God is very KIND;
one of a KIND;
KIND of exceptional
in everyway.

Ll

God is LOVE.
We are expressions of God's boundless LOVE.
God's son Jesus is the LIGHT of the world.
Jesus asks us to let our LIGHTS shine too.

So in that way, let your light shine before all men, that they may see your good deeds and glorify your father in Heaven.
-Mt 5:16

Mm

God is
MAGNIFICENT, MIGHTY,
MAJESTIC, and MERCIFUL.
God is like
a loving MOTHER who
holds us close to her heart.

Be merciful,
just as your Father
is merciful.
Lk 6:36

Nn

God is
NEVER-ENDING.
God always was
and
always will be.

The Lord
reigns as King
forever.
Ps 29:10

God is
OUTSTANDING
and OMNIPOTENT;
that means his
power and authority
are unlimited.

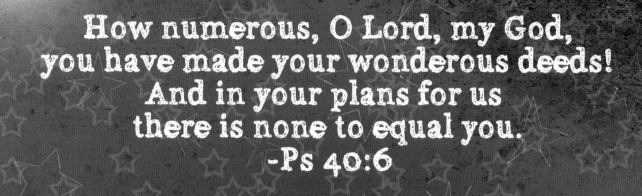

How numerous, O Lord, my God,
you have made your wonderous deeds!
And in your plans for us
there is none to equal you.
-Ps 40:6

Pp

God is PERFECT, POWERFUL, always PRESENT, most PERSISTENT, and PRECIOUS in our sight. God is worthy of all our PRAISE. God is our PROTECTOR.

Keep me as the apple of your eye; hide me in the shadow of your wings from the violence of the wicked. Ps 17:8.9

Qq

God is QUALIFIED to be our God because God can do everything. God can be found in the QUIETEST moment and in the loudest QUAKE. God knows all the answers to every QUESTION we might have.

Bless the Lord who counsels me. Ps 16:7

Amen,
I say to you,
today you will
be with me in
Paradise.
Lk 23:43

Rr

God is our REFUGE
(that means God keeps us safe)
and God is RIGHT
and God
REIGNS over all the Earth.
God promises us
a REWARD in heaven.

Ss

God is our SALVATION,
our SAVING grace,
and our SHEPHERD.
God gives us His Holy SPIRIT to
guide, inspire, and STRENGTHEN us.
God is SPECTACULAR.

**The Lord
is my Shepherd;
there is nothing
I shall want.
Ps 23:1**

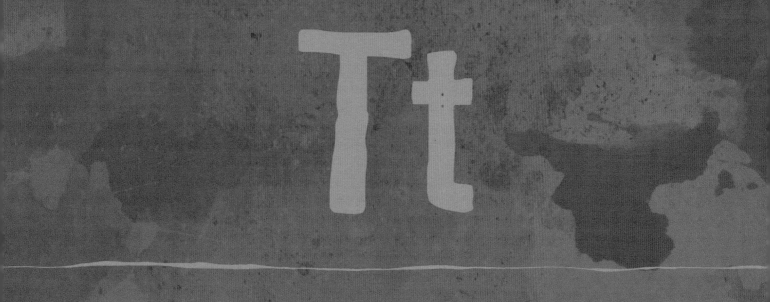

Tt

God is TRUTH.
God deserves
our TIME, our TRUST,
and our THANKSGIVING.

For the Lord's
word is true;
all his works
are trustworthy.
Ps 33:4

Uu

God is UNIVERSAL
(for all people of all times in all places)
and surpasses all UNDERSTANDING.
Even though we keep trying,
we cannot really express
all that God is.

In truth,
I see now that to God,
every person is the same.
God accepts anyone
who worships Him
and does what is right.
Acts 10:34-35

Vv

God is
VICTORIOUS.
No one can outsmart
or overrule God.

Why do you
seek the
living one
among the dead?
He is not here,
but he has been
RAISED.
Lk 24:5,6

In the LORD
I take refuge.
Ps 11:1

Ww

God is
WONDERFUL.
God is in the
WIND and WATER.
God is
WHEREVER
you need God to be.

Xx

God is
EXACT in all things.
God is
EXTRA-SPECIAL
and
EXCEPTIONAL.

Though the grass withers and the flower wilts, the word of our God stands FOREVER.
Is 40:8

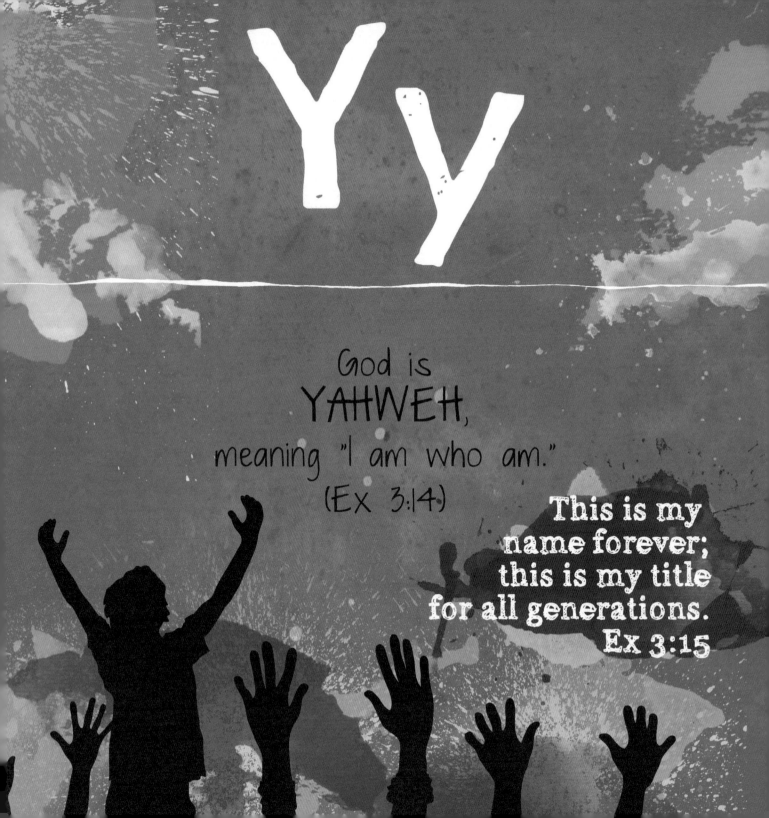

Yy

God is
YAHWEH,
meaning "I am who am."
(Ex 3:14)

This is my
name forever;
this is my title
for all generations.
Ex 3:15

Zz

God is
the source of our
ZEAL and ZEST
for all of life.

You have made known
to me the paths of life;
you will fill me with
joy in your presence.
Acts 2:28

INTRODUCING THE AUTHOR

Peggy Wescott wears many hats:
friend, daughter, sister, wife, mother,
and proud grandmother of eleven exceptional grandchildren.
She is a retired Director of Religious Education
and a certified spiritual director.
She resides in Flushing, Michigan with her husband, Gary.
The ABC's of God is her second children's book.

INTRODUCING THE ILLUSTRATOR

Mallory is a Hillsdale College graduate with a degree in Art.
She lives in Flushing Michigan and
enjoys producing art to glorify the Lord.
Her work is meant to bring a smile to the viewers' face
and is created to inspire hope and love.
Art is her way of expressing her love of God
and her love of the world around her.
The ABC's of God is her second illustrated work.

17031238R00022

Made in the USA
Charleston, SC
23 January 2013